AMERICA'S ELECTORAL COLLEGE
CHOOSING THE PRESIDENT

★————————★

Comparing and Analyzing Charts, Graphs, and Tables

Therese Shea

PowerMath™

The Rosen Publishing Group's
PowerKids Press™
New York

Published in 2007 by The Rosen Publishing Group, Inc.
29 East 21st Street, New York, NY 10010

Book Design: Michael Tsanis

Photo Credits: Cover (hand with ballot box) © The Image Bank; cover (flag background) © Eyewire;
p. 5 (top) © Eric Freeland/Corbis SABA; p. 5 (bottom) © Ron Sachs/Corbis; pp. 7 (both images),
13 (John Adams), 14 (Thomas Jefferson, Aaron Burr) © Bettmann/Corbis; p. 10 © National Archives and
Records Administration; p. 13 (George Washington) © Francis G. Mayer/Corbis; p. 13 (*Journal of the
Senate*); p. 15 © Reuters/Corbis.

Library of Congress Cataloging-in-Publication Data

Shea, Therese.
  America's Electoral College : choosing the President comparing and analyzing charts, graphs, and tables /
Therese Shea.
      p. cm. — (Math for the real world)
  Includes index.
  ISBN 1-4042-3358-X (lib. bdg.)
  ISBN 1-4042-6069-2 (pbk.)
  6-pack ISBN 1-4042-6070-6
  1. Elections—United States—Mathematical models—Juvenile literature. 2. Elections—United States—
Juvenile literature. 3. Elections—United States—History—Juvenile literature. I. Title. II. Series.

  JK1978.S475 2006
  324.6'0973—dc22

                                    2005015701

Manufactured in the United States of America

Contents

The United States Presidential Election

During any United States presidential election, you will hear the term "electoral college." Maybe you have wondered how this "college" affects the outcome of the presidential election.

The electoral college is not a place. It is a system of electing the nation's president and vice president. When citizens of the United States vote for president and vice president, they are actually voting for representatives from the candidates' **political party**. These representatives, called electors, will elect the president and vice president. Normally, electors vote for their own party's candidates.

Each presidential election has 2 results: the popular vote and the electoral vote. The popular vote is the voters' choice for president and vice president. The electoral vote is the electors' choice. The electoral vote decides the presidency and vice presidency. This system was put in place by the founding fathers of the United States in the U.S. Constitution.

Why doesn't the popular vote decide the election? Has the electoral college ever elected a president and vice president who did not win the popular vote? In this book, we'll find the answers to these questions and examine some of the most famous U.S. election results. We'll do this using some of the favorite tools of people who study elections: charts, graphs, and tables. These tools provide an effective way to present complex information so that it is clear and easy to read.

The top picture shows a voting center in New York City on election day—November 7, 2000. The bottom picture shows the U.S. House Chamber during the electoral vote count on January 6, 2001. Except in very close elections, the popular vote results are counted the day of the presidential election in November.

Building a Strong Government

The founding fathers had a big problem to solve at the **Constitutional Convention** of 1787—how to choose their president. Some wanted a single power to govern the colonies as they had been governed under English rule. But they had to be sure the person elected would act in the nation's interests.

There was a great debate about whether the central, or federal, government or the states' governments should hold the most power in the new nation. States worried that the federal government would not let them have enough say about laws within their boundaries. Many people felt more loyalty to their state than to the young nation. However, those favoring a strong federal government believed laws could be passed more easily and the country's interests would be better represented if more power were held in a central government. This was related to another debate about the presidential election. Should Congress or the people have the power to decide the presidency?

The idea of Congress selecting the president caused some concerns. Many felt that each state congressional representative would likely vote for candidates from their state so that their state would benefit most from the president's power. This would lead to a never-ending argument.

At the time of the Constitutional Convention of 1787, shown in the large picture, the founding fathers needed to strengthen the government and the new nation. A strong leader was needed. The inset shows a map of the United States as it looked in 1787.

The convention finally decided that the people should choose the president. This pleased those worried that Congress would have too much power over states. The question then was how people should elect the president. Choosing by a nationwide direct election by **eligible** citizens would lead to each state, again, most likely voting for their candidate. Therefore, the state with the largest population would win, leaving smaller states with no chance for their candidates.

Another concern was that voters would not know much about candidates from other states. Many people could not read or write. At that time, news and information were not easily spread. People often could not travel to hear news or to cast a vote. The founding fathers decided that citizens needed informed representatives.

Look at the bar graph on page 9. A bar graph allows you to compare 2 or more sets of data. This bar graph shows the approximate populations of white male voters in each state based on the national **census** in 1790. If these people voted for their state's candidate, which state would hold the most power in the presidential election? What is the difference in votes between the 2 states with the most voters?

To answer the first question, locate the state with the most voters. Virginia, with about 63,050 voters, had the most voting power.

To answer the second question, locate the state with the second-highest number—Massachusetts with about 59,890 voters. To find the difference, subtract the number of Massachusetts voters from the number of Virginia voters.

$$\begin{array}{r} 63,050 \\ -\ 59,890 \\ \hline 3,160 \end{array}$$

The difference is about 3,160 votes.

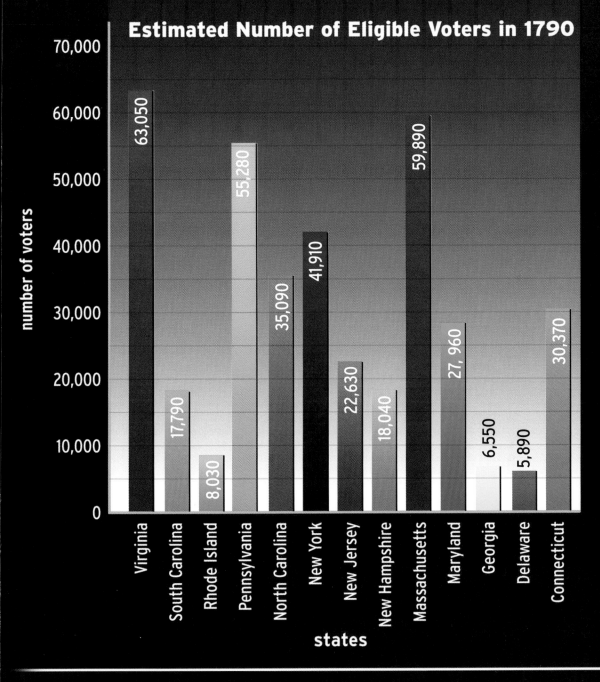

Estimated Number of Eligible Voters in 1790

number of voters

State	Voters
Virginia	63,050
South Carolina	17,790
Rhode Island	8,030
Pennsylvania	55,280
North Carolina	35,090
New York	41,910
New Jersey	22,630
New Hampshire	18,040
Massachusetts	59,890
Maryland	27,960
Georgia	6,550
Delaware	5,890
Connecticut	30,370

states

At this time, most states only allowed white males of a certain age who owned property or paid taxes to vote. Other white males, blacks, women, and Native Americans were not allowed to vote until many years later.

The term "electoral college" is not used in the Constitution, shown here, but it is a term used for the electoral process today. "College" is from the Latin word *collegium*, which means a group in which each member has equal power and authority.

Learning from and Making History

Ancient Romans once used a voting system in which male citizens were divided into groups of 100 according to their wealth. Each group cast 1 vote for or against laws proposed by the Roman Senate. Later, during the **Holy Roman Empire**, a prince from each German state cast a vote for the German king, who then became the emperor. The princes were called "electors."

These ideas helped in forming an electoral system for the United States. The system outlined in the U.S. Constitution had these guidelines:

- Each state has a certain number of electors, equal to the number of its U.S. Senators (2) and the number of its U.S. Representatives (based on the state's population).
- The electors cannot be members of Congress (the Senate or House of Representatives) or a member of the federal government.
- Each state may choose their electors using any method decided by that state's **legislature**.
- Electors must each cast 2 votes for president, but 1 vote must be for a candidate who lives outside their state.
- The winner of the election will be the candidate with the majority of votes—that is, more than $\frac{1}{2}$ of the total votes. The candidate with the second-highest number of votes will become vice president.
- If no candidate receives more than $\frac{1}{2}$ of the votes or if a tie occurs, the U.S. House of Representatives will choose the president from among the 5 candidates with the most electoral votes. Only 1 vote is then cast per state.

After each election, the electoral college votes are sealed and sent to the U.S. Senate. On January 6, each vote is read aloud to the Senate and House of Representatives and the results become official.

In the first U.S. presidential election of 1789, George Washington was the only person who ran for president. All other candidates ran for vice president. The table on page 13 is taken from the *Journal of the Senate* in 1789 after the first presidential election. A table organizes data into columns and rows so information can be easily located. Read over the rules of the electoral college on page 11 again, then answer these questions. According to the table, how many electoral college members were there in 1789? Which state's electors cast the most votes for the man elected vice president?

To answer the first question, first count the total number of votes cast. The number of votes cast for each candidate is listed below the candidates' names. The sum is 138 votes. Since each elector is required to cast 2 votes, divide the total number of votes by 2 to find the number of electors.

138 votes ÷ 2 = number of electors

The total number of electors is 69.

To answer the second question, look at the candidate with the second-largest number of votes: John Adams with 34. In the column under his name, find the largest number of votes: 10. Massachusetts cast the most votes for John Adams, the elected vice president.

George Washington

"*Mr. President:* I am directed by the House of Representatives to inform the Senate, that the House is ready forthwith to meet the Senate, to attend the opening and counting of the votes of the Electors of the President and Vice President of the United States."—And he withdrew.

Ordered, That Mr. Paterson be a teller on the part of the Senate.

The Speaker and the House of Representatives attended in the Senate chamber, for the purpose expressed in the message delivered by by Ellsworth— and after some time withdrew.

The Senate then proceeded by ballot to the choice of a President of their body, pro tempore.

JOHN LANGDON, Esq. was duly elected.

The President elected for the purpose of counting the votes, declared to the Senate, that the Senate and House of Representatives had met, and that he, in their presence, had opened and counted the votes of the electors for President and Vice President of the United States, which were as follow:

STATES.	George Washington, Esq.	John Adams, Esq.	Samuel Huntingdon, Esq.	John Jay, Esq.	John Hancock, Esq.	Robert H. Harrison, Esq.	George Clinton, Esq.	John Rutledge, Esq.	John Milton, Esq.	James Armstrong, Esq.	Edward Telfair, Esq.	Benjamin Lincoln, Esq.
New Hampshire,	5	5	—	—	—	—	—	—	—	—	—	—
Massachusetts,	10	10	—	—	—	—	—	—	—	—	—	—
Connecticut,	7	5	2	—	—	—	—	—	—	—	—	—
New Jersey,	6	1	—	5	—	—	—	—	—	—	—	—
Pennsylvania,	10	8	—	—	2	—	—	—	—	—	—	—
Delaware,	3	—	—	3	—	—	—	—	—	—	—	—
Maryland,	6	—	—	—	—	6	—	—	—	—	—	—
Virginia,	10	5	—	1	1	—	3	—	—	—	—	—
South Carolina,	7	—	—	—	—	—	—	6	—	—	—	—
Georgia,	5	—	—	—	—	—	—	—	2	1	1	1
	69	34	2	9	4	6	3	6	2	1	1	1

Whereby it appears, that

GEORGE WASHINGTON, Esq. was unanimously elected President, and JOHN ADAMS, Esq. was duly elected Vice President, of the United States of America.

Mr. Madison came from the House of Representatives with the following verbal message:

Mr. President: I am directed by the House of Representatives to inform the Senate, that the House have agreed, that the notifications of the election of the President and of the Vice President of the United States, should be made by such persons, and in such manner, as the Senate shall be pleased to direct. And he withdrew.

Whereupon, the Senate appointed Charles Thomson, Esq. to notify George Washington, Esq. of his election to the office of President of the United States of America, and Mr. Sylvanus Bourn to notify John Adams, Esq. of his election to the office of Vice President of the said United States.

The instructions to the messengers are in the following words:

IN SENATE, April 6, 1789.

SIR: The Senate of the United States have appointed you to wait upon General Washington, with a certificate of his being elected to the office of President of the United States of America. You will therefore prepare to set out as soon as possible,

George Washington was the only presidential candidate who ever ran unopposed. He ran again in the election of 1792 with the same results.

John Adams

Unexpected Results

Thomas Jefferson

By 1800, people with similar political views had formed political parties. The chosen electors developed loyalty to these parties. In the election of 1800, the electors loyal to the Democratic-Republican Party gave an equal number of votes to Democratic-Republicans Thomas Jefferson and Aaron Burr. Aaron Burr was actually running for vice president, but he and Jefferson were tied for the most votes and he was therefore in the running for president. As stated in the Constitution, the House of Representatives had to vote on the decision. After 35 votes in which Jefferson received 1 vote less than he needed for the majority, Jefferson was finally chosen as president.

To stop this from happening again, the Twelfth **Amendment** was passed. This stated that each elector would cast 1 vote for president and 1 vote for vice president. As before, 1 candidate had to be from a state other than the state where the elector lived. The House of Representatives would continue to break any tie vote for the presidency, deciding among the 3 candidates with the most electoral votes. The Senate would break a tie if one occurred in the vice-presidential race.

Aaron Burr

ELECTORS FOR PRESIDENT AND VICE PRESIDENT

REPUBLICAN PARTY
GEORGE W. BUSH for President
DICK CHENEY for Vice President　　　4 ➡

DEMOCRATIC PARTY
AL GORE for President
JOE LIEBERMAN for Vice President　　6 ➡

LIBERTARIAN PARTY
HARRY BROWNE for President
ART OLIVIER for Vice President　　8 ➡

GREEN PARTY
RALPH NADER for President
WINONA LaDUKE for Vice President　　10 ➡

SOCIALIST WORKERS PARTY
JAMES HARRIS for President
MARGARET TROWE for Vice President　　12 ➡

NATURAL LAW PARTY
JOHN HAGELIN for President
NAT GOLDHABER for Vice President　　14 ➡

REFORM PARTY
PAT BUCHANAN for President
EZOLA FOSTER for Vice President　　16 ➡

SOCIALIST PARTY
DAVID McREYNOLDS for President
MARY CAL HOLLIS for Vice President　　18 ➡

CONSTITUTION PARTY
HOWARD PHILLIPS for President　　20 ➡

Notice the top of this ballot says "electors for" and then the names of each party and its candidates. Voters choose electors as a group when they cast their vote for their candidate. Names of individual electoral candidates are not often listed on ballots.

To vote for a write-in candidate, follow the directions on the secrecy envelope

If candidates win the nation's popular vote, they will usually win the majority of electors' votes. In the election of 1824, this did not happen.

The Democratic-Republicans presented 4 candidates for president: Andrew Jackson, John Quincy Adams, William Crawford, and Henry Clay. The result—no candidate received enough electoral votes (more than $\frac{1}{2}$ of the 261 total electoral votes) to win the election. Again, the vote went to the House of Representative and each state cast 1 vote for president. John Quincy Adams won the majority of the House votes.

A pie chart shows partial amounts out of a whole amount. The pie chart on page 17 shows each candidate's share of the popular vote. The bar graph below it shows the electoral votes in the election of 1824. Based on the pie chart, who won the popular vote? Based on the bar graph, who had the most electoral votes?

To find the winner of the popular vote, find the candidate who has the largest "piece" of the pie chart. The candidate with 41.3% of the vote was Andrew Jackson.

To find the candidate with the most electoral votes, locate the candidate with the tallest bar on the graph—Andrew Jackson.

Jackson had the most popular votes and electoral votes. However, he did not have the majority of electoral votes needed to win the election—131.

All of the presidential candidates in the election of 1824 were from the same party. The Federalist Party had ceased to exist prior to the election. Today, each party chooses 1 presidential candidate and 1 vice-presidential candidate to run for election.

Popular Vote in the 1824 Presidential Election

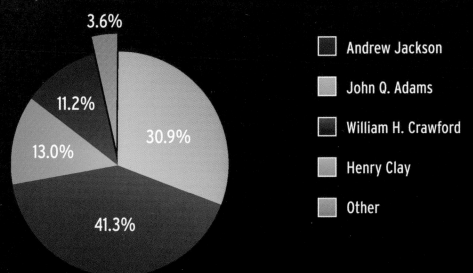

3.6%

11.2%

13.0%

30.9%

41.3%

- Andrew Jackson
- John Q. Adams
- William H. Crawford
- Henry Clay
- Other

Electoral Votes in the 1824 Presidential Election

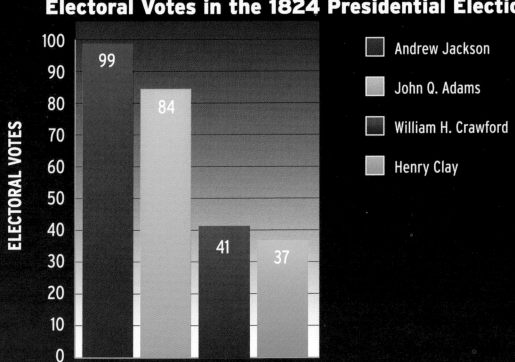

ELECTORAL VOTES

99

84

41

37

- Andrew Jackson
- John Q. Adams
- William H. Crawford
- Henry Clay

The Winner-Takes-All Tradition

Each political party usually chooses people who are loyal to their party to run as electors. The U.S. Constitution allows states to decide how to choose their electors. All states except Maine and Nebraska choose their electors through a statewide election by the people.

When a citizen votes for presidential and vice-presidential candidates on a ballot, they are actually voting for a party's electors. The voter understands the electors will vote for their party's candidate. For example, a Democrat would vote for Democratic electors, who would then vote for the Democratic candidate. Although it rarely happens, electors may choose not to vote according to the popular vote or for their party's candidate.

Except Nebraska and Maine, every state has a tradition called "winner-takes-all." This means the winners of the majority of the popular vote get all the state's electoral votes. So, if the Republican party won the popular vote in a state, all electors would be Republicans and would vote for the Republican candidates. Usually the popular vote and the electoral vote agree, but this did not happen in the elections of 1888 and 2000.

In Maine and Nebraska, 2 electors are chosen by statewide popular vote and others are chosen by popular vote in each congressional district, an area represented by a member of the House of Representatives. These maps show the population densities of Nebraska and Maine. How might voting for electors by congressional district help people in less-populated areas?

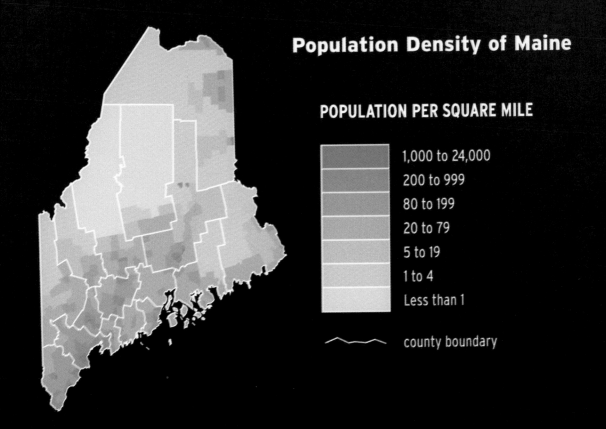

Population Density of Maine

POPULATION PER SQUARE MILE

- 1,000 to 24,000
- 200 to 999
- 80 to 199
- 20 to 79
- 5 to 19
- 1 to 4
- Less than 1

— county boundary

POPULATION PER SQUARE MILE

- 1,000 to 15,100
- 200 to 999
- 80 to 199
- 20 to 79
- 5 to 19
- 1 to 4
- Less than 1

— county boundary

Population Density of Nebraska

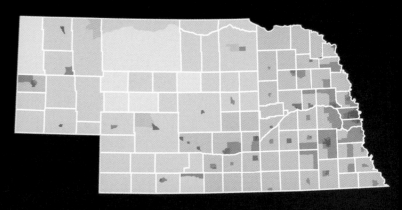

Election Results of 1888

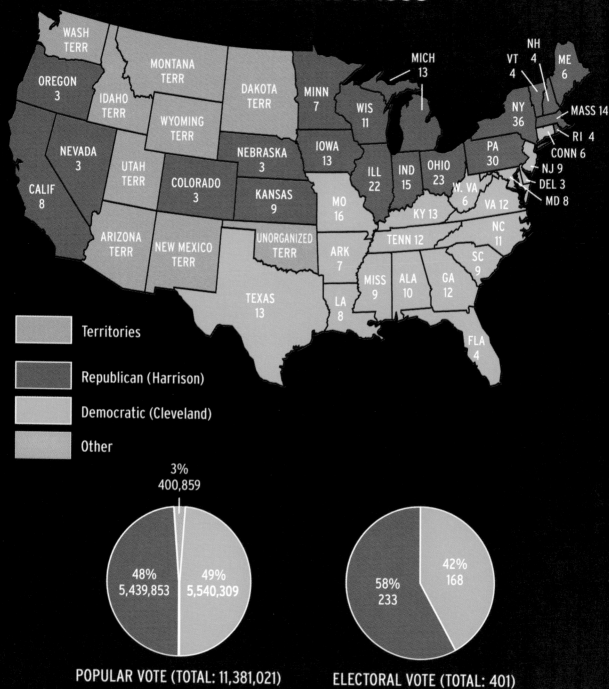

WASH TERR	
OREGON 3	
IDAHO TERR	
MONTANA TERR	
DAKOTA TERR	
MINN 7	
WIS 11	
MICH 13	
NH 4	VT 4	ME 6
NEVADA 3	
UTAH TERR	
WYOMING TERR	
NEBRASKA 3	
IOWA 13	
ILL 22	IND 15	OHIO 23
PA 30	NY 36	MASS 14
CALIF 8	
COLORADO 3	
KANSAS 9	
MO 16	
KY 13	
W. VA 6	VA 12	RI 4	CONN 6	NJ 9	DEL 3	MD 8
ARIZONA TERR	NEW MEXICO TERR	
UNORGANIZED TERR	
ARK 7	
TENN 12	
NC 11	SC 9
TEXAS 13	
LA 8	MISS 9	ALA 10	GA 12
FLA 4	

Legend:
- Territories
- Republican (Harrison)
- Democratic (Cleveland)
- Other

POPULAR VOTE (TOTAL: 11,381,021)
- 3% 400,859
- 48% 5,439,853
- 49% 5,540,309

ELECTORAL VOTE (TOTAL: 401)
- 58% 233
- 42% 168

Conflicting Votes:
A Look at 2 Elections

Republican Benjamin Harrison ran for president in 1888 against **incumbent** Democratic president Grover Cleveland. Compare the 2 pie charts on page 20 to find the election results. Who won the popular vote? Who won the electoral vote?

Cleveland won the popular vote by a slim amount, but Harrison won the electoral vote. How could this happen? Even though Harrison won the popular vote in many states, he won by only a small number of votes. Two states decided the election: Indiana and New York. These states are called swing states, since they are not strongly loyal to either a candidate or a party. The results in those states may "swing" to any candidate. Harrison won the popular vote in both of these states. Through the winner-takes-all system, he also won the large number of electoral votes in each state.

Look at the election result map and pie charts on page 20. Each state's number of electoral votes is noted on the map. If Cleveland had won the electoral votes in Indiana and New York, how many total electoral votes would he have had?

To find this answer, locate the 2 swing states on the map. Add the number of electoral votes each had. Indiana had 15 votes and New York had 36 votes for a total of 51 votes. Now find the number of votes that Cleveland had (168) and add that to the total votes in the swing states.

$$\begin{array}{r} 15 \text{ votes} \\ +36 \text{ votes} \\ \hline 51 \text{ votes} \end{array} \qquad \begin{array}{r} 168 \text{ votes} \\ +51 \text{ votes} \\ \hline 219 \text{ votes} \end{array}$$

Cleveland would have had 219 total electoral votes if he had won the 2 swing states. This is more than $\frac{1}{2}$ of the total electoral votes. He would have won the election.

In the election of 2000, the 2 chief candidates were incumbent vice president Al Gore Jr., a Democrat, and George W. Bush, a Republican. Usually, **analysts** know the outcome of the election when the polls close because of the winner-takes-all tradition. Figures counted for 47 states and the District of Columbia gave 246 electoral votes to Bush and 255 electoral votes to Gore. The number of electoral votes needed to win was 270 votes. In 3 states—New Mexico, Oregon, and Florida—the popular vote was too close to predict the outcome. Florida, with 25 electoral votes, would give either man enough votes to be elected. New Mexico and Oregon together had only 12 votes, not enough to give either candidate a victory.

Florida law **mandates** recounting the ballots if the popular vote is close. After the recount, Bush was ahead of Gore by only 537 votes. Gore asked the Florida Supreme Court for ballots to be recounted in heavily Democratic counties. Bush then asked the United States Supreme Court, the nation's highest court, to stop the recount. The U.S. Supreme Court ruling on December 12 favored Bush. The judges did not stop the recount, but they stated that 1 person should be in charge of the recounting procedures and all recounting should be done using the same methods. There was not time to set up a system, so the numbers had to stand. George W. Bush had won the presidency.

This map shows that winning the support of most states doesn't guarantee winning the election by a large majority. Although Bush won many states, he received only 5 more electoral votes than Gore received. Use the map on page 23 and the text above to find the total number of electoral votes that each candidate received after the results came in from New Mexico, Oregon, and Florida. (Subtract 1 vote from Gore since 1 of the 3 electors for Washington, D.C., decided not to vote.)

Election Results of 2000

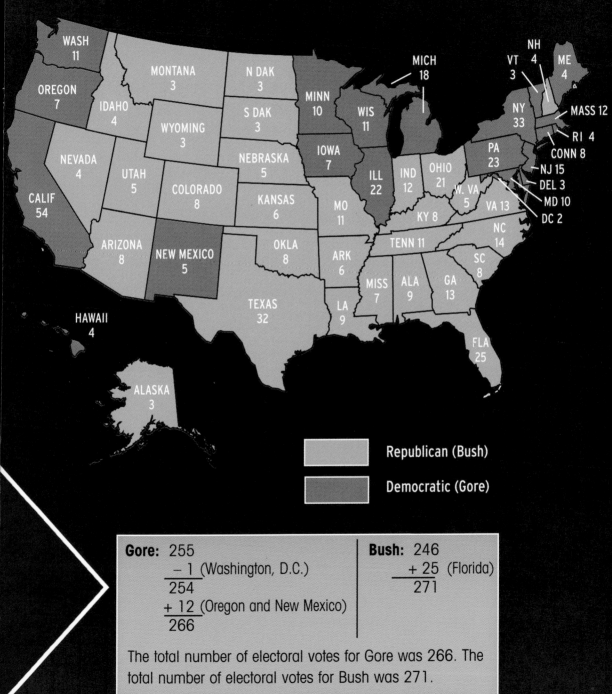

State	Votes
WASH	11
OREGON	7
MONTANA	3
IDAHO	4
NEVADA	4
UTAH	5
WYOMING	3
CALIF	54
ARIZONA	8
NEW MEXICO	5
COLORADO	8
N DAK	3
S DAK	3
NEBRASKA	5
KANSAS	6
OKLA	8
TEXAS	32
HAWAII	4
ALASKA	3
MINN	10
IOWA	7
MO	11
ARK	6
LA	9
WIS	11
ILL	22
MICH	18
IND	12
OHIO	21
KY	8
TENN	11
MISS	7
ALA	9
GA	13
W. VA	5
VA	13
NC	14
SC	8
FLA	25
PA	23
NY	33
VT	3
NH	4
ME	4
MASS	12
RI	4
CONN	8
NJ	15
DEL	3
MD	10
DC	2

Republican (Bush)

Democratic (Gore)

Gore: 255
   − 1 (Washington, D.C.)
   ———
   254
   + 12 (Oregon and New Mexico)
   ———
   266

Bush: 246
   + 25 (Florida)
   ———
   271

The total number of electoral votes for Gore was 266. The total number of electoral votes for Bush was 271.

Debating the Electoral College

After the 2000 presidential election, more people began questioning the electoral college. Do we need it now that citizens can more easily educate themselves about each candidate? Do we need it now that there are better methods of directly casting our votes? What is the purpose of the electoral college today?

People against the process say it was put in place because the founding fathers did not believe citizens were educated enough to vote. They argue that every citizen should have the right to vote directly for a candidate. Putting too much power in the hands of the electors takes the power away from the voter. They argue that the winner-takes-all system does not fairly reflect the people's choice. If 49% of a state's population cast their ballots for 1 candidate and 51% voted for another, in most states the candidate with 51% would win all electoral votes. In this case, 49% of the people—nearly $\frac{1}{2}$—would be denied their candidate.

Also, some states have an advantage over other states because they have more electors. Often, candidates spend more time campaigning in states with many electors. As we saw in the election of 2000, 3 states were in question at the end of the election, but only 1 state "mattered."

In the 2004 election, George W. Bush ran for reelection against Massachusetts senator John Kerry, a Democrat, and Independent candidate Ralph Nader. These pie charts show the results of an exit poll, which is a survey of voters as they leave their voting location.

CANDIDATE	POPULAR VOTE	VOTE %	ELECTORAL VOTE
R BUSH (Incumbent)	62,040,606	51%	286
D KERRY	59,028,109	48%	252
I NADER	411,304	1%	0

Vote by Party

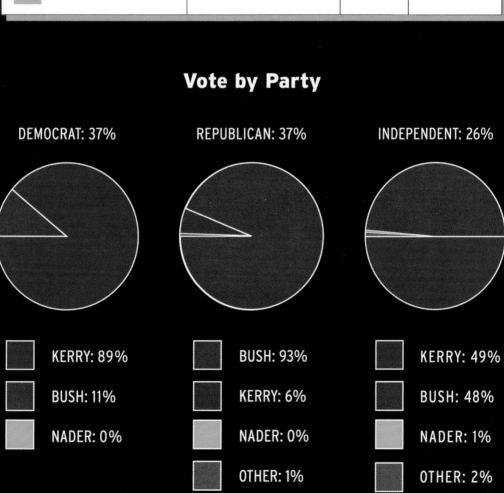

DEMOCRAT: 37%

KERRY: 89%
BUSH: 11%
NADER: 0%

REPUBLICAN: 37%

BUSH: 93%
KERRY: 6%
NADER: 0%
OTHER: 1%

INDEPENDENT: 26%

KERRY: 49%
BUSH: 48%
NADER: 1%
OTHER: 2%

Electoral college supporters say the system is fairer than a direct popular vote. In a direct election, the most populated areas of the country could elect a president while less-populated areas would have little power. Supporters have suggested ways of changing the electoral college to make it a fair reflection of the popular vote.

One idea is to expand the House of Representatives, which would increase the number of electors. Each state has a number of electors equal to the number of senators (2) plus the number of U.S. Representatives. The last time the House was expanded in 1911, each member represented 212,000 citizens. Currently, each member represents about 674,000 citizens. If more representatives were added and each elector voted according to a district, voters might be better represented.

Every 10 years, after the country's census, the number of representatives to the House may be reduced in a state, decreasing the number of electors, or increased, increasing the number of electors. The table on page 27 shows the number of electoral votes allowed to each state in the periods following 2 censuses. Which states' populations increased the most from the first census to the second? Which states' populations decreased the most?

To find the states with the greatest increase in population, look for the states in which numbers of electors increased from the first census to the second census. The states that gained the most electors were Arizona, Florida, Georgia, and Texas, which each gained 2 electors.

To find the states with the greatest decrease in population, look for the states that lost the most electors. New York and Pennsylvania each lost 2 electors.

State	after 1990 census	after 2000 census
Alabama	9	9
Alaska	3	3
Arizona	8	10
Arkansas	6	6
California	54	55
Colorado	8	9
Connecticut	8	7
Delaware	3	3
D.C.	3	3
Florida	25	27
Georgia	13	15
Hawaii	4	4
Idaho	4	4
Illinois	22	21
Indiana	12	11
Iowa	7	7
Kansas	6	6
Kentucky	8	8

State	after 1990 census	after 2000 census
Louisiana	9	9
Maine	4	4
Maryland	10	10
Massachusetts	12	12
Michigan	18	17
Minnesota	10	10
Mississippi	7	6
Missouri	11	11
Montana	3	3
Nebraska	5	5
Nevada	4	5
New Hampshire	4	4
New Jersey	15	15
New Mexico	5	5
New York	33	31
North Carolina	14	15
North Dakota	3	3
Ohio	21	20

State	after 1990 census	after 2000 census
Oklahoma	8	7
Oregon	7	7
Pennsylvania	23	21
Rhode Island	4	4
South Carolina	8	8
South Dakota	3	3
Tennessee	11	11
Texas	32	34
Utah	5	5
Vermont	3	3
Virginia	13	13
Washington	11	11
West Virginia	5	5
Wisconsin	11	10
Wyoming	3	3

Total Number of Electors: 538

The number of representatives in the House has remained at 435 since 1911. Since each state has a number of electors equal to its number of senators (2) plus its number of representatives, that makes 535 electors. Washington, D.C., was granted 3 electoral votes in the Twenty-third Amendment to the Constitution, making the total number of electors 538.

In the past 200 years, over 700 proposals have been made to change or get rid of the electoral college. However, changing the U.S. Constitution is a difficult process. To add an amendment, $\frac{2}{3}$ of the House of Representatives and the Senate need to approve it, as well as $\frac{3}{4}$ of the state legislatures.

Recently, another change has been discussed by state legislatures regarding the winner-takes-all tradition. Each state is allowed to choose its electors in any way it wants. Only Maine and Nebraska do not follow the winner-takes-all system. Other states could also choose their electors in a different way. An elector could be chosen by each **congressional district**, meaning that each group of people represented by a U.S. representative could choose an elector. If $\frac{1}{2}$ of the state voted in favor of one candidate and the other $\frac{1}{2}$ voted for another, the votes could be split.

The graph on page 29 is a scatter plot. A scatter plot shows relationships among data. In this graph, the 11 most populated states are placed on the graph according to their population and number of electoral votes. This scatter plot shows that the number of electoral votes in each state increases as population increases. Which state has the largest population and therefore the greatest number of votes? You should have chosen California, which has a population of over 33 million people and has 55 electoral votes. Can you find which 3 states each have the same number of electoral votes? How many more electoral votes does California have than each of these 3 states has?

Comparing State Populations and Electoral Votes

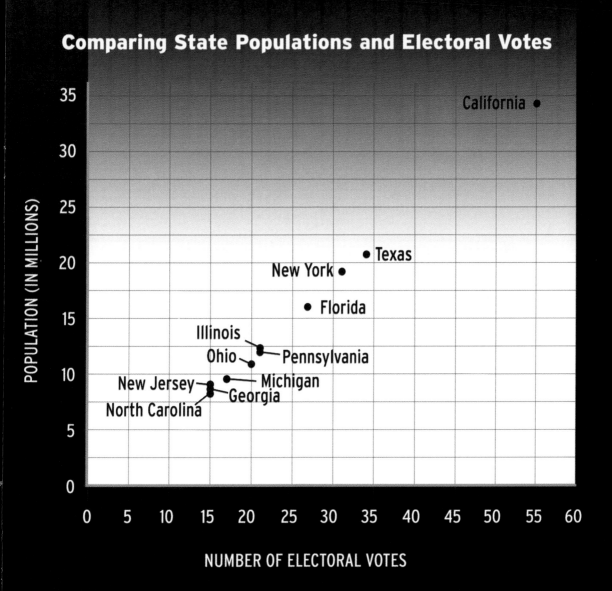

POPULATION (IN MILLIONS) / **NUMBER OF ELECTORAL VOTES**

California
Texas
New York
Florida
Illinois
Ohio
Pennsylvania
New Jersey
Michigan
Georgia
North Carolina

Under the current system, if a candidate wins the 11 highly populated states shown here, the candidate will win enough electoral votes to win the presidency even if the remaining 38 states and Washington, D.C., cast their electoral votes for the opposing candidate.

Participating in the Democratic Process

The electoral college does not take the power of the vote completely out of the hands of voting citizens. Each vote at the poll counts toward the popular vote, which determines how the electors will vote.

The line graph below shows that fewer young people are voting in presidential elections. Perhaps they do not believe 1 person can make a difference in a country as large as the United States. They need only look at the election of 2000. The final vote in a country of over 290 million people was decided by a few hundred votes, perhaps fewer than the number of students in your school. The right to vote is not granted to people in all countries. Learning about the election process and participating in your country's government is a responsibility and a privilege.

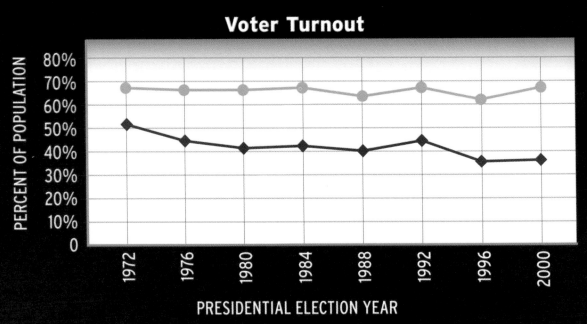

Voter Turnout

Glossary

amendment (uh-MEND-muhnt) An official change to the U.S. Constitution.

analyst (AA-nuh-luhst) Someone who studies the elements of something and how they relate to each other.

census (SEHN-suhs) A count of a population. In the United States, it occurs every 10 years.

congressional district (kuhn-GREH-shuh-nuhl DIHS-trikt) A division of a state from which a member of the U.S. House of Representatives is elected.

Constitutional Convention (kahn-stuh-TOO-shuh-nuhl kuhn-VEHN-shun) A meeting held in 1787 by the founding fathers of the United States. During this meeting, state delegates drew up a new plan of government—the Constitution of the United States.

eligible (EH-luh-juh-buhl) Qualified to participate.

Holy Roman Empire (HOH-lee ROH-muhn EHM-pyr) The name given to the empire of German and Italian territories that existed from the A.D. 900s until 1806.

incumbent (in-KUHM-buhnt) Occupying a specific office, such as that of president of the United States.

legislature (LEH-juhs-lay-chuhr) A group of people elected to make laws.

mandate (MAN-dayt) To require.

political party (puh-LIH-tih-kuhl PAHR-tee) An organization of people involved in politics and government who share the same political views.

Index

America's Electoral College,
    choosing the President :
Author: Shea, Therese.
Reading Level: 7.9 MG
Point Value: 1.0
ACCELERATED READER QUIZ 108017